wn

Sounds & Letters 17

T0025483

KNOWLEDGE BOOKS

whale	wheat
wheel	wheelbarrow
wheelchair	whirlpool
whisper	

wh

whale

wheat

wheel

wheelbarrow

wheelchair

whirlpool

whisper

15

whale	wheat
wheel	wheelbarrow
wheelchair	whirlpool
whisper	

Knowledge Books and Software

PO Box 50 Sandgate, Queensland 4017 Australia
p. +617-55680288 f. +617-55680277 email: sales@kbs.com.au

First Published 2022
ISBN 9781922516893
Text and editing: Carole Crimeen
Design and layout: Suzanne Fletcher
Publisher: Robert Watts

Series Information: **Sounds and Letters**

Credits

Photographs: Cover © ANURAK PONGPATIMET; p. 1 © Richard Peterson, Geiger, M.fowers, Photo Melon; p. 3 © Xavier MARCHANT; p. 5 © Frolova_Elena; p. 7 © Den Rozhnovsky; p. 9 © ElenaY; p. 11 © siraphat; p. 13 © M.fowers; p. 15 © Photo Melon/Shutterstock.

Phonic support books are a wonderful resource for emergent readers as they encourage independent reading and help students make the link between letters and the sounds they represent.

Have students identify the images on the title page to listen for the sound that they will hear through the book.

Encourage students to point to each word as they read through the book.

ISBN: 9781922516893

9 781922 516893 >

KNOWLEDGE BOOKS